Knock, Knock
Jokes!

Other Smarties titles available

Smarties Beautiful Beasties
Smarties Book of Wizardry
Smarties Chuckle Factory
Smarties Deadly Dinosaurs
Smarties Dinosaur Jokes
Smarties Hairy Humans
Smarties Hilariously Funny Verse
Smarties How to Draw Cartoons
Smarties How to Make 'Em Laugh Joke Book
Smarties Joke Book
Smarties Puzzle Busters
Smarties Smart Art
Smarties Smart Science
Smarties Travel Teasers
Smarties Wacky World

Nestlé SMARTIES
Knock, Knock Jokes

Robinson Children's Books

Constable & Robinson Ltd
3 The Lanchesters
162 Fulham Palace Road
London
W6 9ER

First published in the UK by Robinson Children's Books,
an imprint of Constable & Robinson Ltd, 2001

A copy of the British Library Cataloguing in Publication Data
for this title is available from the British Library

ISBN 1-84119-411-5

Printed and bound in the EC

10 9 8 7 6 5 4 3 2 1

Contents

Girls   1

Boys   71

Zoo's There?   137

All Around the World   155

What's for Dinner?   174

Famous People   191

Bits and Bodies   199

Ring! Ring!   206

Pick a Colour   210

Whoooo's There   214

Teacher! Teacher!   221

Sing a Song   225

Double Trouble   235

Lucky Dip   239

Girls

Knock, knock.
Who's there?
Abbey.
Abbey who?
Abbey new year!

Knock, knock.
Who's there?
Ada.
Ada who?
You're Ada your mind!

Knock, knock.
Who's there?
Adina.
Adina who?
Adina is served!

Knock, knock.
Who's there?
Agatha.
Agatha who?
Agatha splitting
headache.

Knock, knock.
Who's there?
Agrippa.
Agrippa who?
Agrippa before she escapes!

Knock, knock.
Who's there?
Aida.
Aida who?
Aida let me in if I were you.

Knock, knock.
Who's there?
Aleta.
Aleta who?
Aleta from the postman.

Knock, knock.
Who's there?
Alf.
Alf who?
Alf all if you don't catch me!

3

Knock, knock.
Who's there?
Alice.
Alice who?
Alice fair in love and war!

Knock, knock.
Who's there?
Alison.
Alison who?
Alison Wonderland.

Knock, knock.
Who's there?
Alka.
Alka who?
Alka Pone.

Knock, knock.
Who's there?
Alma.
Alma who?
Alma-ny times do I have to knock?

4

Knock, knock.
Who's there?
Althea.
Althea who?
Althea in court.

Knock, knock.
Who's there?
Amana May.
Amana May who?
Amana May holidays!

Knock, knock.
Who's there?
Amana.
Amana who?
Amana-eating tiger!

Knock, knock.
Who's there?
Amanda.
Amanda who?
Amanda fix the
refrigerator is here.

Knock, knock.
Who's there?
Amanda Lynn.
Amanda Lynn who?
Amanda Lynn is like
a guitar.

Knock, knock.
Who's there?
Amber.
Amber who?
Amber-sting to go to the
bathroom.

Knock, knock.
Who's there?
Amelia.
Amelia who?
Amelia letter yesterday.

Knock, knock.
Who's there?
Amy.
Amy who?
Amy body home?

Knock, knock.
Who's there?
Anais.
Anais who?
Anais cup of tea!

Knock, knock.
Who's there?
Anana.
Anana who?
Anana split.

Knock, knock.
Who's there?
Anastasia.
Anastasia who?
Anastasia until you open
the door.

Knock, knock.
Who's there?
Anemone.
Anemone who?
Anemone is not a friend.

Knock, knock.
Who's there?
Anita.
Anita who?
Anita see you, open
the door!

Knock, knock.
Who's there?
Anita Loos.
Anita Loos who?
Anita Loos about 20lbs

Knock, knock.
Who's there?
Ann.
Ann who?
Ann Tartic

Knock, knock.
Who's there?
Anna.
Anna who?
Anna Rack.

Knock, knock.
Who's there?
Anna Mary.
Anna Mary who?
Anna Mary old soul
was he . . .

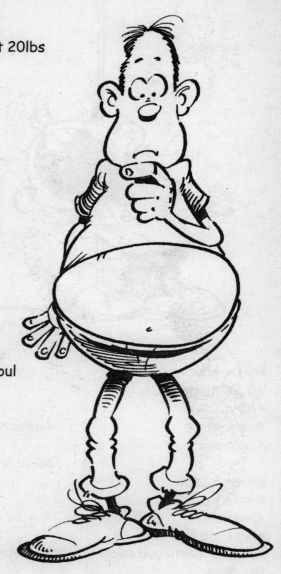

Knock, knock.
Who's there?
Annie.
Annie who?
Annie one you like.

Knock, knock.
Who's there?
Anthea.
Anthea who?
Anthea pants.

Knock, knock.
Who's there?
Anya.
Anya who?
Anya gonna let me in, or what?

Knock, knock.
Who's there?
Anya.
Anya who?
Anya Lee!

Knock, knock.
Who's there?
Aretha.
Aretha who?
Aretha to the end of
the street!

Knock, knock.
Who's there?
Audrey.
Audrey who?
Audrey 'nother drink.

Knock, knock.
Who's there?
Barbara.
Barbara who?
Barbara of Seville!

Knock, knock.
Who's there?
Bea.
Bea who?
Bea love and open
the door.

Knock, knock.
Who's there?
Belladonna.
Belladonna who?
Belladonna work, so I
had to knock!

Knock, knock.
Who's there?
Belle Lee.
Belle Lee who?
Belle Lee dancer!

Knock, knock.
Who's there?
Belle.
Belle who?
Belle-t up and open
the door.

Knock, knock.
Who's there?
Bertha.
Bertha who?
Bertha day girl.

11

Knock, knock.
Who's there?
Beryl.
Beryl who?
Beryl nice to come in!

Knock, knock.
Who's there?
Beryl Lee.
Beryl Lee who?
Beryl Lee able to reach
the bell!

Knock, knock.
Who's there?
Beth.
Beth who?
Beth foot forward.

Knock, knock.
Who's there?
Bettina.
Bettina who?
Bettina minute you'll
open the door.

Knock, knock.
Who's there?
Betty B.
Betty B. who?
Betty B. careful!

Knock, knock.
Who's there?
Bronwen.
Bronwen who?
Bronwen are you going to
open the door?

Knock, knock.
Who's there?
Buffy.
Buffy who?
Buffy-t are killig be and
I've got a stinkig cold!

Knock, knock.
Who's there?
Camilla.
Camilla who?
Camilla, lights, action!

13

Knock, knock.
Who's there?
Candice.
Candice who?
Candice be really happening?

Knock, knock.
Who's there?
Carina.
Carina who?
Carina ditch, can I have a lift?

Knock, knock.
Who's there?
Carmen.
Carmen who?
Carmen get it!

Knock, knock.
Who's there?
Carmencita.
Carmencita who?
Carmencita down and have
a rest!

Knock, knock.
Who's there?
Carol.
Carol who?
Carol go if you get some petrol.

Knock, knock.
Who's there?
Carrie.
Carrie who?
Carrie me home, I'm tired.

Knock, knock.
Who's there?
Carrie R.
Carrie R. who?
Carrie R. pigeon.

Knock, knock.
Who's there?
Celeste.
Celeste who?
Celeste time I lend you money.

15

Knock, knock.
Who's there?
Celia.
Celia who?
Celia later alligator.

Knock, knock.
Who's there?
Celia May.
Celia May who?
Celia May, I forgot my keys!

Knock, knock.
Who's there?
Charlotta.
Charlotta who?
Charlotta fuss about nothing!

Knock, knock.
Who's there?
Chelsea.
Chelsea who?
Chelsea what I can do.

16

Knock, knock.
Who's there?
Cher.
Cher who?
Cher and share alike!

Knock, knock.
Who's there?
Chloe.
Chloe who?
Chloe encounters of the
third kind.

Knock, knock.
Who's there?
Cherry.
Cherry who?
OK, see you later.

Knock, knock.
Who's there?
Cindy.
Cindy who?
Cindy next one in!

Knock, knock.
Who's there?
Clara.
Clara who?
Clara space on the table.

Knock, knock.
Who's there?
Clara Lee.
Clara Lee who?
Clara Lee you haven't
a clue!

Knock, knock.
Who's there?
Clarissa.
Clarissa who?
Clarissa, Clarissa, come
Clarissa!

Knock, knock.
Who's there?
Claudette.
Claudette who?
Claudette a whole cake.

Knock, knock.
Who's there?
Claudia.
Claudia who?
Claudia eyes out!

Knock, knock.
Who's there?
Colleen.
Colleen who?
Make a Colleen break!

Knock, knock.
Who's there?
Courtney.
Courtney who?
Courtney robbers lately?

Knock, knock.
Who's there?
Cynthia.
Cynthia who?
You've grown Cynthia
last time I saw you!

Knock, knock.
Who's there?
Daisy.
Daisy who?
Daisy that you are in, but I don't believe them.

Knock, knock.
Who's there?
Dana.
Dana who?
Dana talk with your mouth full.

Knock, knock.
Who's there?
Danielle.
Danielle who?
Danielle at me, it's not my fault!

Knock, knock.
Who's there?
Dawn.
Dawn who?
Dawn do anything
I wouldn't do.

Knock, knock.
Who's there?
Desiree.
Desiree who?
Desiree doctor in the house?

Knock, knock.
Who's there?
Diana.
Diana who?
Diana thirst. Get me
some water.

Knock, knock.
Who's there?
Diane.
Diane who?
Diane to meet you!

Knock, knock.
Who's there?
Diaz.
Diaz who?
Diaz of our lives!

Knock, knock.
Who's there?
Dolores.
Dolores who?
Dolores an ass.

Knock, knock.
Who's there?
Donalette.
Donalette who?
Donalette it get you down!

Knock, knock.
Who's there?
Dona Lewis.
Dona Lewis who?
Dona Lewis touch!

Knock, knock.
Who's there?
Dora.
Dora who?
Dora Steel.

Knock, knock.
Who's there?
Dorothy.
Dorothy who?
Dorothy wheels on a
tricycle.

Knock, knock.
Who's there?
Eartha.
Eartha who?
Eartha me again and I'll
tell you.

Knock, knock.
Who's there?
Dot.
Dot who?
Dot really care.

Knock, knock.
Who's there?
Edith.
Edith who?
Edith eat taken?

23

Knock, knock.
Who's there?
Edna.
Edna who?
Edna clouds.

Knock, knock.
Who's there?
Effie.
Effie who?
Effie'd known you were
coming he'd have stayed
home.

Knock, knock.
Who's there?
Eileen.
Eileen who?
Eileen-d over and fell.

Knock, knock.
Who's there?
Elizabeth.
Elizabeth who?
Elizabeth of knowledge
is a dangerous thing.

Knock, knock.
Who's there?
Emma.
Emma who?
Emma glad you asked
me that!

Knock, knock.
Who's there?
Ellen.
Ellen who?
Ellen high water.

Knock, knock.
Who's there?
Emma Lou King.
Emma Lou King who?
Emma Lou King through
the letterbox!

Knock, knock.
Who's there?
Elsie.
Elsie who?
Elsie you in court!

25

Knock, knock.
Who's there?
Enid.
Enid who?
Enid to use your bathroom.

Knock, knock.
Who's there?
Erda.
Erda who?
Erda cows.

Knock, knock.
Who's there?
Esme.
Esme who?
Esme, let me in!

Knock, knock.
Who's there?
Esther.
Esther who?
Esther anything I can do for you?

Knock, knock.
Who's there?
Etta.
Etta who?
Etta big cake.

Knock, knock.
Who's there?
Eva.
Eva who?
Eva had a smack in the mouth?

Knock, knock.
Who's there?
Evadne.
Evadne who?
Evadne complaints?

Knock, knock.
Who's there?
Eve.
Eve who?
Eve-ho, here we go.

Knock, knock.
Who's there?
Evi.
Evi who?
Evi-thing's coming up
roses.

Knock, knock.
Who's there?
Faith.
Faith who?
Faith to Faith.

Knock, knock.
Who's there?
Fergie.
Fergie who?
Fergieness sake let
me in!

Knock, knock.
Who's there?
Fanny.
Fanny who?
Fanny you not knowing
who I am!

Knock, knock.
Who's there?
Faye.
Faye who?
Faye Kit.

Knock, knock.
Who's there?
Fiona.
Fiona who?
Fiona large house and a
car.

Knock, knock.
Who's there?
Flora.
Flora who?
Flora no particular
reason.

Knock, knock.
Who's there?
Fiona Lee.
Fiona Lee who?
Fiona Lee you'd let me in,
I'll tell you!

Knock, knock.
Who's there?
Freda.
Freda who?
Freda, she was
locked up.

29

Knock, knock.
Who's there?
Gaynor.
Gaynor who?
Gaynor couple of pounds.

Knock, knock.
Who's there?
Geri.
Geri who?
Geri-lly want to know?

Knock, knock.
Who's there?
Germaine.
Germaine who?
Germaine you don't
recognize me?

Knock, knock.
Who's there?
Gertie.
Gertie who?
Gertiesy call.

Knock, knock.
Who's there?
Grace.
Grace who?
Grace your knee.

Knock, knock.
Who's there?
Gita.
Gita who?
Gita job!

Knock, knock.
Who's there?
Gladys.
Gladys who?
Gladys letter isn't a bill.

Knock, knock.
Who's there?
Gretyl.
Gretyl who?
Gretyl's boiled, make me
a cup of tea!

Knock, knock.
Who's there?
Guinevere.
Guinevere who?
Guinevere going to get together?

Knock, knock.
Who's there?
Gwen.
Gwen who?
Gwen will I see you again?

Knock, knock.
Who's there?
Gwynn N.
Gwynn N. who?
Gwynn N. bear it!

Knock, knock.
Who's there?
Hailey.
Hailey who?
Hailey Tosis!

Knock, knock.
Who's there?
Hannah.
Hannah who?
Hannah the rotten knock, knock joke!

Knock, knock.
Who's there?
Harriet.
Harriet who?
Harriet up!

Knock, knock.
Who's there?
Hartley.
Hartley who?
Speak up, I can Hartley hear you!

Knock, knock.
Who's there?
Hayley.
Hayley who?
Hayley me alone can't you?

Knock, knock.
Who's there?
Heather.
Heather who?
Heather-nother cake.

Knock, knock.
Who's there?
Heather Lee.
Heather Lee who?
Stop breathing so
Heather Lee!

Knock, knock.
Who's there?
Hedda.
Hedda who?
Hedda ball over here.

Knock, knock.
Who's there?
Heidi Claire.
Heidi Claire who?
Heidi Claire war.

Knock, knock.
Who's there?
Hermione.
Hermione who?
Hermione is made up and
I can't change it!

Knock, knock.
Who's there?
Holly.
Holly who?
Holly Lujah!

Knock, knock.
Who's there?
Hester.
Hester who?
Hester la vista!

Knock, knock.
Who's there?
Ida Kline.
Ida Kline who?
Ida Kline to answer
that question!

Knock, knock.
Who's there?
Iona Lee.
Iona Lee who?
Iona Lee called to say
hello!

Knock, knock.
Who's there?
Irene.
Irene who?
Irene and Irene but still
no one answers.

Knock, knock.
Who's there?
Iris.
Iris who?
Iris you would open
the door.

Knock, knock.
Who's there?
Iris May.
Iris May who?
Iris May case, Your
Honour!

Knock, knock.
Who's there?
Irma.
Irma who?
Irma Lergic!

Knock, knock.
Who's there?
Isabel.
Isabel who?
Isabel necessary on a
bicycle?

Knock, knock.
Who's there?
Isadore.
Isadore who?
Isadore right to
come in?

Knock, knock.
Who's there?
Isla.
Isla who?
Isla be seeing you!

Knock, knock.
Who's there?
Izzy.
Izzy who?
Izzy come, Izzy go.

Knock, knock.
Who's there?
Jackie.
Jackie who?
Jackie is under the mat!

Knock, knock.
Who's there?
Jackie T.
Jackie T. who?
Jackie T. and tie!

Knock, knock.
Who's there?
Jan.
Jan who?
Jan sandwich.

Knock, knock.
Who's there?
Jane.
Jane who?
Jane-bar of Secrets.

Knock, knock.
Who's there?
Janet.
Janet who?
Janet a big fish?

Knock, knock.
Who's there?
Jasmine.
Jasmine who?
Jasmine, give it back!

Knock, knock.
Who's there?
Jean.
Jean who?
Jeanius – you just don't recognize it.

Knock, knock.
Who's there?
Jenny.
Jenny who?
Jenny-d anything from
the shops?

Knock, knock.
Who's there?
Jess.
Jess who?
Don't know, you tell me.

Knock, knock.
Who's there?
Jess B.
Jess B. who?
Jess B. Cuzz.

Knock, knock.
Who's there?
Joan.
Joan who?
Joan call us, we'll
call you.

Knock, knock.
Who's there?
Joanna.
Joanna who?
Joanna open the door
and let me in?

Knock, knock.
Who's there?
Josette.
Josette who?
Josette here and I'll
sit there.

Knock, knock.
Who's there?
Joanna Lee
Joanna Lee who?
Joanna Lee open on
weekdays?

Knock, knock.
Who's there?
Judy.
Judy who?
Judy-liver newspapers?

41

Knock, knock.
Who's there?
Juliet.
Juliet who?
Juliet him get away with that?

Knock, knock.
Who's there?
Juno.
Juno who?
I dunno, Juno?

Knock, knock.
Who's there?
Justine.
Justine who?
Justine the nick of time.

Knock, knock.
Who's there?
Karen.
Karen who?
Karen the can for you.

Knock, knock.
Who's there?
Kay.
Kay who?
Kay sera sera.

Knock, knock.
Who's there?
Kristin.
Kristin who?
Kristin Gown.

Knock, knock.
Who's there?
Lauren.
Lauren who?
Lauren order.

Knock, knock.
Who's there?
Leslie.
Leslie who?
Leslie this sleepy town!

Knock, knock.
Who's there?
Lisa.
Lisa who?
Lisa falling from the trees!

Knock, knock.
Who's there?
Liz-Anne.
Liz-Anne who?
Liz-Anne to me when I'm speaking!

Knock, knock.
Who's there?
Louise.
Louise who?
Louise the second on the right!

Knock, knock.
Who's there?
Lucille.
Lucille who?
Lucille the envelope and
I'll post it!

Knock, knock.
Who's there?
Lucy.
Lucy who?
Lucy Nupp!

Knock, knock.
Who's there?
Lulu.
Lulu who?
Lulu's not working, can I use yours?

Knock, knock.
Who's there?
Mabel.
Mabel who?
Mabel doesn't work either.

Knock, knock.
Who's there?
Ma Belle.
Ma Belle who?
Ma Belle E. aches.

Knock, knock.
Who's there?
Madge Ickle.
Madge Ickle who?
Madge Ickle Mystery
Tour.

Knock, knock.
Who's there?
Mae.
Mae who?
Mae be I'll tell you,
maybe I won't.

Knock, knock.
Who's there?
Mahatma.
Mahatma who?
Mahatma Kote.

Knock, knock.
Who's there?
Mandy.
Mandy who?
Mandy lifeboats.

Knock, knock.
Who's there?
Marcella.
Marcella who?
Marcella is flooded with water!

Knock, knock.
Who's there?
Mary.
Mary who?
Mary Christmas.

Knock, knock.
Who's there?
Mariah.
Mariah who?
Mariah me!

Knock, knock.
Who's there?
Maya.
Maya who?
Maya turn next.

Knock, knock.
Who's there?
May Kay.
May Kay who?
May Kay while the sun
shines!

Knock, knock.
Who's there?
Megan.
Megan who?
Megan other cup of
coffee.

Knock, knock.
Who's there?
Mel.
Mel who?
Mel Aria.

Knock, knock.
Who's there?
Michelle.
Michelle who?
Michelle suit is very
shiny.

Knock, knock.
Who's there?
Millicent.
Millicent who?
Millicent me over to
knock on your door!

Knock, knock.
Who's there?
Mindy.
Mindy who?
Mindy fresh breath!

Knock, knock.
Who's there?
Misha.
Misha who?
Misha lot of things while
I was away.

Knock, knock.
Who's there?
Moira.
Moira who?
The Moira the merrier!

Knock, knock.
Who's there?
Monica.
Monica who?
Monica-s have fallen down!

Knock, knock.
Who's there?
Nadia.
Nadia who?
Nadia head if you want to come in.

Knock, knock.
Who's there?
Nancy.
Nancy who?
Nancy a piece of cake?

Knock, knock.
Who's there?
Nell.
Nell who?
Nell of the ball.

Knock, knock.
Who's there?
Noreen.
Noreen who?
Noreen on this bone!

Knock, knock.
Who's there?
Norma Lee.
Norma Lee who?
Norma Lee I'd call before I came over.

Knock, knock.
Who's there?
Nunya.
Nunya who?
Nunya business.

Knock, knock.
Who's there?
Olga.
Olga who?
Olga home shall I?

Knock, knock.
Who's there?
Olive.
Olive who?
Olive me alone.

Knock, knock.
Who's there?
Olivia.
Olivia who?
Olivia, let me in!

Knock, knock.
Who's there?
Onya.
Onya who?
Onya marks, get set, GO!

Knock, knock.
Who's there?
Orla.
Orla who?
Orla lights just went
out!

Knock, knock.
Who's there?
Peg.
Peg who?
Peg your pardon, wrong house.

Knock, knock.
Who's there?
Phyllida.
Phyllida who?
Phyllida bucket of water.

Knock, knock.
Who's there?
Philippa.
Philippa who?
Philippa bath – I'm really dirty.

Knock, knock.
Who's there?
Polly.
Polly who?
Polly other one, it's got bells on.

Knock, knock.
Who's there?
Poppy.
Poppy who?
Poppy in any time you
like.

Knock, knock.
Who's there?
Portia.
Portia who?
Portia the door – it's
stuck.

Knock, knock.
Who's there?
Renata.
Renata who?
Renata money. Can I
borrow some?

Knock, knock.
Who's there?
Rhonda.
Rhonda who?
Rhonda arrest!

Knock, knock.
Who's there?
Rita.
Rita who?
Rita my lips!

Knock, knock.
Who's there?
Roxanne.
Roxanne who?
Roxanne stones all over
the place.

Knock, knock.
Who's there?
Rose.
Rose who?
Rose of chairs.

Knock, knock.
Who's there?
Ruth.
Ruth who?
Ruth is leaking again!

55

Knock, knock.
Who's there?
Sabina.
Sabina who?
Sabina long time since I've seen you!

Knock, knock.
Who's there?
Sacha.
Sacha who?
Sacha fuss, just because I knocked on
the door!

Knock, knock.
Who's there?
Sadie.
Sadie who?
Sadie magic words!

Knock, knock.
Who's there?
Sally.
Sally who?
Sally everything
you own.

Knock, knock.
Who's there?
Sandy.
Sandy who?
Sandy Beach!

Knock, knock.
Who's there?
Sarah.
Sarah who?
Sarah reason you're not laughing?

Knock, knock.
Who's there?
Shania.
Shania who?
Shania-s place you've got here.

Knock, knock.
Who's there?
Sharon.
Sharon who?
Sharon share alike.

Knock, knock.
Who's there?
Sheila.
Sheila who?
Sheila be wearing pink
pyjamas when she comes!

Knock, knock.
Who's there?
Shelley Cohn.
Shelley Cohn who?
Shelly Cohn Carne.

Knock, knock.
Who's there?
Shirley.
Shirley who?
Shirley you know who I
am!

Knock, knock.
Who's there?
Sigrid.
Sigrid who?
Sigrid Service, open up!

Knock, knock.
Who's there?
Sonia.
Sonia who?
Sonia shoe, it stinks!

Knock, knock.
Who's there?
Stephanie Lee.
Stephanie Lee who?
Stephanie Lee something
fishy going on!

Knock, knock.
Who's there?
Stephanie.
Stephanie who?
Stephanie gas – we need
to go faster!

Knock, knock.
Who's there?
Stella.
Stella who?
Stella later, shall we?

Knock, knock.
Who's there?
Sue.
Sue who?
Sue-prise, it's me!

Knock, knock.
Who's there?
Sue King.
Sue King who?
Sue King wet!

Knock, knock.
Who's there?
Suzanne.
Suzanne who?
Suzanne Sox!

Knock, knock.
Who's there?
Sybil.
Sybil who?
Sybil-ing rivalry.

Knock, knock.
Who's there?
Tabatha.
Tabatha who?
Tabatha baby, test the
water with your elbow.

Knock, knock.
Who's there?
Tamara.
Tamara who?
Tamara is Tuesday.

Knock, knock.
Who's there?
Tamara May
Tamara May who?
Tamara May never come!

Knock, knock.
Who's there?
Tamsin.
Tamsin who?
Tamsin time again I
come to the wrong
house.

Knock, knock.
Who's there?
Tania.
Tania who?
Tania life around.

Knock, knock.
Who's there?
Tara.
Tara who?
Tara very much!

Knock, knock.
Who's there?
Tara Lee.
Tara Lee who?
I'm Tara Lee exhausted!

Knock, knock.
Who's there?
Tess Slater.
Tess Slater who?
Tess Slater than you think!

Knock, knock.
Who's there?
Thea.
Thea who?
Thea later, alligator.

Knock, knock.
Who's there?
Thea King.
Thea King who?
Heat Thea King missile!

Knock, knock.
Who's there?
Theo.
Theo who?
Theo Shun.

Knock, knock.
Who's there?
Theresa.
Theresa who?
Theresa Green.

Knock, knock.
Who's there?
Tilly.
Tilly who?
Tilly cows come home.

Knock, knock.
Who's there?
Tina.
Tina who?
Tina tuna.

Knock, knock.
Who's there?
Tori.
Tori who?
Tori to disturb you.

Knock, knock.
Who's there?
Tracy.
Tracy who?
Tracy paper.

Knock, knock.
Who's there?
Trudy.
Trudy who?
Trudy your word.

Knock, knock.
Who's there?
Valencia.
Valencia who?
Valencia fiver?

Knock, knock.
Who's there?
Uta May.
Uta May who?
I'm going Uta May mind!

Knock, knock.
Who's there?
Vanessa.
Vanessa who?
Vanessa time you need
me, I'll be there!

Knock, knock.
Who's there?
Vera.
Vera who?
Vera you been?

Knock, knock.
Who's there?
Wanda.
Wanda who?
Wanda what took you so
long?

Knock, knock.
Who's there?
Wendy.
Wendy who?
Wendy last time you had
a bath?

Knock, knock.
Who's there?
Whitney.
Whitney who?
Whitney have to say
to me?

Knock, knock.
Who's there?
Willow.
Willow who?
Willow let me in!

Knock, knock.
Who's there?
Wilma.
Wilma who?
Wilma dinner be ready
soon?

Knock, knock.
Who's there?
Xena.
Xena who?
Xena minute!

Knock, knock.
Who's there?
Yoko.
Yoko who?
Yoko jump in the lake.

Knock, knock.
Who's there?
Yolande.
Yolande who?
Yolande me a fiver and I'll pay you back.

Knock, knock.
Who's there?
Yvette.
Yvette who?
Yvette do you want?

Knock, knock.
Who's there?
Yvonne.
Yvonne who?
Yvonne to come in?

Knock, knock.
Who's there?
Zelda.
Zelda who?
Zelda second-hand car.

Knock, knock.
Who's there?
Zizi.
Zizi who?
Zizi when you know how.

Knock, knock.
Who's there?
Zoe.
Zoe who?
Zoe meet again!

Boys

Knock, knock.
Who's there?
Aaron.
Aaron who?
Aaron your chest!

Knock, knock.
Who's there?
Abel.
Abel who?
Abel to open the door,
or not?

Knock, knock.
Who's there?
Abbott.
Abbott who?
Abbott time you opened
the door!

Knock, knock.
Who's there?
Adam.
Adam who?
Adam-sel in distress.

Knock, knock.
Who's there?
Adonai.
Adonai who?
Adonai kebab with chilli
sauce.

Knock, knock.
Who's there?
Alan Dew.
Alan Dew who?
Alan Dew some money.

Knock, knock.
Who's there?
Adrian.
Adrian who?
Adrian full of dirty
water.

Knock, knock.
Who's there?
Alan.
Alan who?
Alan in a day's work.

Knock, knock.
Who's there?
Albee.
Albee who?
Albee here when you
open the door.

Knock, knock.
Who's there?
Albert.
Albert who?
Albert you'll never
guess.

Knock, knock.
Who's there?
Alcott.
Alcott who?
Alcott the cake.

Knock, knock.
Who's there?
Aldo.
Aldo who?
Aldo the washing up.

Knock, knock.
Who's there?
Aldous.
Aldous who?
Aldous who agree stand up!

Knock, knock.
Who's there?
Alec.
Alec who?
Alec to come in.

Knock, knock.
Who's there?
Alex.
Alex who?
Alex plain later.

Knock, knock.
Who's there?
Alfie.
Alfie who?
Alfie you later, alligator!

Knock, knock.
Who's there?
Alf Lee.
Alf Lee who?
Alf Lee sorry, wrong house!

Knock, knock.
Who's there?
Alfred.
Alfred who?
Alfred this joke before!

Knock, knock.
Who's there?
Alistair.
Alistair who?
Alistair's in this house are broken.

Knock, knock.
Who's there?
Amahl.
Amahl who?
Amahl Function!

Knock, knock.
Who's there?
Amos.
Amos who?
Amosquito.

Knock, knock.
Who's there?
Anatola.
Anatola who?
Anatola bridge.

Knock, knock.
Who's there?
Archer.
Archer who?
Archer glad I knocked?

Knock, knock.
Who's there?
Archie.
Archie who?
Bless you!

Knock, knock.
Who's there?
Ariel.
Ariel who?
You're Ariel pain in
the neck.

Knock, knock.
Who's there?
Arthur.
Arthur who?
Arthur Mometer.

Knock, knock.
Who's there?
Arnie.
Arnie who?
Arnie you gonna invite
me in?

Knock, knock.
Who's there?
Arthur Hugh
Arthur Hugh who?
Arthur Hugh than me!

Knock, knock.
Who's there?
Artie Fish.
Artie Fish who?
Artie Fish L.
Intelligence.

Knock, knock.
Who's there?
Ashley.
Ashley who?
Ashley I don't care.

Knock, knock.
Who's there?
Atilla.
Atilla who?
Atilla you no lies.

Knock, knock.
Who's there?
Aubrey.
Aubrey who?
Aubrey quiet!

Knock, knock.
Who's there?
Barbie.
Barbie who?
Barbie Q.

Knock, knock.
Who's there?
Ben Hur.
Ben Hur who?
Ben Hur an hour – let me in.

Knock, knock.
Who's there?
Ben.
Ben who?
Ben down and tie your
shoelaces.

Knock, knock.
Who's there?
Barry.
Barry who?
Barry this bone, doggy.

Knock, knock.
Who's there?
Benjamin.
Benjamin who?
Benjamin the blues.

Knock, knock.
Who's there?
Bill.
Bill who?
Bill-tup area.

Knock, knock.
Who's there?
Bjorn.
Bjorn who?
Bjorn free.

Knock, knock.
Who's there?
Bobby.
Bobby who?
Bobby-n up and down.

Knock, knock.
Who's there?
Bob Dwyer.
Bob Dwyer who?
Bob Dwyer on your fence,
I ripped my trousers!

Knock, knock.
Who's there?
Boris.
Boris who?
Boris stiff.

Knock, knock.
Who's there?
Brad.
Brad who?
Brad news, I'm afraid!

Knock, knock.
Who's there?
Brent.
Brent who?
Brent out of shape.

Knock, knock.
Who's there?
Brook.
Brook who?
Brook me a ticket.

Knock, knock.
Who's there?
Bruce.
Bruce who?
Bruce a pretty boy then?

Knock, knock.
Who's there?
Bruno.
Bruno who?
Bruno who it is!

Knock, knock.
Who's there?
Buster.
Buster who?
Buster the town centre
please.

Knock, knock.
Who's there?
Cain.
Cain who?
Cain tell you.

Knock, knock.
Who's there?
Carl.
Carl who?
Carl get you there
quicker than walking.

Knock, knock.
Who's there?
Callum.
Callum who?
Callum names!

Knock, knock.
Who's there?
Carlo.
Carlo who?
Carlo taxi!

Knock, knock.
Who's there?
Chad.
Chad who?
Chad you could come.

Knock, knock.
Who's there?
Chandler.
Chandler who?
Chandler with care!

Knock, knock.
Who's there?
Chester.
Chester who?
Chester drawers.

Knock, knock.
Who's there?
Chuck.
Chuck who?
Chuck mate!

Knock, knock.
Who's there?
Clive.
Clive who?
Clive aboard and enjoy
the ride!

Knock, knock.
Who's there?
Clarence.
Clarence who?
Clarence Sale.

Knock, knock.
Who's there?
Claud.
Claud who?
Claud Nine!

Knock, knock.
Who's there?
Cole.
Cole who?
Cole as a cucumber.

Knock, knock.
Who's there?
Colin.
Colin who.
Colin and see me sometime.

Knock, knock.
Who's there?
Craig.
Craig who?
Craig in the wall!

Knock, knock.
Who's there?
Cyril.
Cyril who?
Cyril pleasure to meet you!

Knock, knock.
Who's there?
Dale.
Dale who?
Dale come if you call 'em.

Knock, knock.
Who's there?
Dan.
Dan who?
Dan Druff.

Knock, knock.
Who's there?
Danny.
Danny who?
Dannybody home?

Knock, knock.
Who's there?
Darius.
Darius who?
Darius something I need to say.

Knock, knock.
Who's there?
Darren.
Darren who?
Darren you to let me in!

Knock, knock.
Who's there?
Daryl.
Daryl who?
Daryl be the day.

Knock, knock.
Who's there?
Dave Finn.
Dave Finn who?
Dave Finn-ately.

Knock, knock.
Who's there?
Dennis.
Dennis who?
Dennis says I need a
tooth out!

Knock, knock.
Who's there?
Desi.
Desi who?
Desi want a drink?

Knock, knock.
Who's there?
Dexter.
Dexter who?
Dexter halls with boughs
of holly!

Knock, knock.
Who's there?
Don Blaine.
Don Blaine who?
Don Blaine me, I'm just
following orders!

Knock, knock.
Who's there?
Don.
Don who?
Don leave me this way.

Knock, knock.
Who's there?
Don Boris Witty.
Don Boris Witty who?
Don Boris Witty details!

Knock, knock.
Who's there?
Duane.
Duane who?
Duane the bathwater.

Knock, knock.
Who's there?
Duke.
Duke who?
Duke come here often?

Knock, knock.
Who's there?
Dunbar.
Dunbar who?
Dunbar the door, I'll climb through a window!

Knock, knock.
Who's there?
Duncan.
Duncan who?
Duncan biscuits in your coffee.

Knock, knock.
Who's there?
Dustin.
Dustin who?
Dustin the nick of time!

Knock, knock.
Who's there?
Dwight.
Dwight who?
Dwight way and da
wrong way.

Knock, knock.
Who's there?
Eamon.
Eamon who?
Eamon a good mood —
have my piece of cake.

Knock, knock.
Who's there?
Earl.
Earl who?
Earl tell you if you open
the door.

Knock, knock.
Who's there?
Eddie.
Eddie who?
Eddie-body home?

Knock, knock.
Who's there?
Edward.
Edward who?
Edward be nice to come in.

Knock, knock.
Who's there?
Egbert.
Egbert who?
Egbert no bacon.

Knock, knock.
Who's there?
Egon.
Egon who?
Egon toast!

Knock, knock.
Who's there?
Elia.
Elia who?
Elia wake all night.

Knock, knock.
Who's there?
Emil.
Emil who?
Emil would be nice, can I stay for dinner?

Knock, knock.
Who's there?
Emmett.
Emmett who?
Emmett the other door.

Knock, knock.
Who's there?
Enoch.
Enoch who?
Enoch and Enoch but there's no answer!

Knock, knock.
Who's there?
Erin.
Erin who?
Erin your nostrils.

Knock, knock.
Who's there?
Esau.
Esau who?
Esau you in the bath!

Knock, knock.
Who's there?
Eustace.
Eustace who?
Come Eustace you are!

Knock, knock.
Who's there?
Evan.
Evan who?
Evan only knows!

Knock, knock.
Who's there?
Ewan.
Ewan who?
No, just me.

Knock, knock.
Who's there?
Felix.
Felix who?
Felix my ice cream, I'll
lick his!

Knock, knock.
Who's there?
Ezra.
Ezra who?
Ezra room to rent?

Knock, knock.
Who's there?
Fido.
Fido who?
Fido known you were
coming I'd have baked
a cake.

Knock, knock.
Who's there?
Fitzherbert.
Fitzherbert who?
Fitzherbert-er than it
fits me.

Knock, knock.
Who's there?
Fitzhugh.
Fitzhugh who?
Fitzhugh better than it
fits her and me.

Knock, knock.
Who's there?
Fletcher.
Fletcher who?
Fletcher stick, there's a
good dog.

Knock, knock.
Who's there?
Frank Lee.
Frank Lee who?
Frank Lee, it's none of
your business!

Knock, knock.
Who's there?
Fletcher.
Fletcher who?
Fletcher self go.

Knock, knock.
Who's there?
Frank.
Frank who?
You're welcome.

Knock, knock.
Who's there?
Franz.
Franz who?
Franz, Romans,
countrymen, lend me
your ears.

Knock, knock.
Who's there?
Frazier.
Frazier who?
Frazier going through.

Knock, knock.
Who's there?
Fred.
Fred who?
Fred I've got some bad news.

Knock, knock.
Who's there?
Freddie.
Freddie who?
Freddie needle with cotton.

Knock, knock.
Who's there?
Galahad.
Galahad who?
Galahad my last biscuit!

Knock, knock.
Who's there?
Gary.
Gary who?
Gary on the
good work!

Knock, knock.
Who's there?
Geoff.
Geoff who?
Geoff feel like
letting me in?

Knock, knock.
Who's there?
Gerald.
Gerald who?
Gerald friend again!

Knock, knock.
Who's there?
Gino.
Gino who?
Yes, it's me of course!

Knock, knock.
Who's there?
Giovanni.
Giovanni who?
Giovanni more cake?

Knock, knock.
Who's there?
Guiseppe.
Guiseppe who?
Guiseppe some dog muck!

Knock, knock.
Who's there?
Gus.
Gus who?
That's what you're
supposed to do!

Knock, knock.
Who's there?
Hank.
Hank who?
Don't mention it!

Knock, knock.
Who's there?
Hans.
Hans who?
Hans off the table!

Knock, knock.
Who's there?
Harry.
Harry who?
Harry up and open
the door!

Knock, knock.
Who's there?
Harold.
Harold who?
Harold do you think
I am?

Knock, knock.
Who's there?
Harvey.
Harvey who?
Harvey going to the
cinema tonight?

Knock, knock.
Who's there?
Herman.
Herman who?
Herman dry.

Knock, knock.
Who's there?
Hiram.
Hiram who?
Hiram and fire 'em.

Knock, knock.
Who's there?
Holmes.
Holmes who?
Holmes where the heart is.

Knock, knock.
Who's there?
Horace.
Horace who?
Horace I to know you
live here?

103

Knock, knock.
Who's there?
Horatio.
Horatio who?
Horatio to the end of
the road.

Knock, knock.
Who's there?
Howard.
Howard who?
Howard you like to open
the door?

Knock, knock.
Who's there?
Howie.
Howie who?
Howie Dewin?

Knock, knock.
Who's there?
Huey.
Huey who?
Huey too much!

Knock, knock.
Who's there?
Hugh.
Hugh who?
Hugh coming outside?

Knock, knock.
Who's there?
Ike.
Ike who?
Ike-n see you through the keyhole.

Knock, knock.
Who's there?
I.M. Holden.
I.M. Holden who?
I.M. Holden my breath.

Knock, knock.
Who's there?
Isaac.
Isaac who?
Isaac all my staff today!

Knock, knock.
Who's there?
Ivan.
Ivan who?
Ivan my money back.

Knock, knock.
Who's there?
Jamie.
Jamie who?
Jamie-n you don't recognize me?

Knock, knock.
Who's there?
Jason.
Jason who?
Jason a rainbow.

Knock, knock.
Who's there?
Jeffrey.
Jeffrey who?
Jeffrey time I knock, you won't open the door.

Knock, knock.
Who's there?
Jerry.
Jerry who?
Jerry trifle.

Knock, knock.
Who's there?
Jethro.
Jethro who?
Jethro our ball back please?

Knock, knock.
Who's there?
Jim.
Jim who?
Jim mind if I come in?

Knock, knock.
Who's there?
Jimmy.
Jimmy who?
Jimmy all your money.

Knock, knock.
Who's there?
Jock.
Jock who?
Jock late cake!

Knock, knock.
Who's there?
John Q.
John Q. who?
You're welcome.

Knock, knock.
Who's there?
John.
John who?
John the dots!

Knock, knock.
Who's there?
Jordan.
Jordan who?
Jordan know who I am?

108

Knock, knock.
Who's there?
Joshua.
Joshua who?
Joshua opening the door
yesterday, I ran off!

Knock, knock.
Who's there?
Joss.
Joss who?
Joss you wait and see!

Knock, knock.
Who's there?
Juan.
Juan who?
Juan of those things.

Knock, knock.
Who's there?
Justin.
Justin who?
Justin Case.

Knock, knock.
Who's there?
Keanu.
Keanu who?
Keanu lend me a fiver?

Knock, knock.
Who's there?
Keith.
Keith who?
Keith your hands off me!

Knock, knock.
Who's there?
Keith.
Keith who?
Keith me, thweetheart!

Knock, knock.
Who's there?
Kent.
Kent who?
Kent see without
my glasses.

Knock, knock.
Who's there?
Kerry.
Kerry who?
Kerry Erbag.

Knock, knock.
Who's there?
Lance.
Lance who?
Lance Lide!

Knock, knock.
Who's there?
Lee King.
Lee King who?
Lee King roof.

Knock, knock.
Who's there?
Leon.
Leon who?
Leon me – I'll support you.

Knock, knock.
Who's there?
Les.
Les who?
Les wait and see.

Knock, knock.
Who's there?
Lesley.
Lesley who?
Lesley-ping dogs lie.

Knock, knock.
Who's there?
Lester.
Lester who?
Lester said the better!

Knock, knock.
Who's there?
Lionel.
Lionel who?
Lionel roar if you stand on its tail.

Knock, knock.
Who's there?
Lloyd.
Lloyd who?
Lloyd a donkey to water.

Knock, knock.
Who's there?
Luke.
Luke who?
Luke through the
keyhole and see.

Knock, knock.
Who's there?
Luke.
Luke who?
Luke out, another knock,
knock joke!

Knock, knock.
Who's there?
Luther.
Luther who?
Luther please – not
so tight!

Knock, knock.
Who's there?
Malcolm.
Malcolm who?
Malcolm from cows.

Knock, knock.
Who's there?
Matthew.
Matthew who?
Matthew lace hath
come undone!

Knock, knock.
Who's there?
Martin.
Martin who?
Martin is full of biscuits!

Knock, knock.
Who's there?
Maurice.
Maurice who?
Maurice better
than less.

Knock, knock.
Who's there?
Max.
Max who?
Max no difference.

Knock, knock.
Who's there?
Michael.
Michael who?
Michael-ock has
stopped ticking.

Knock, knock.
Who's there?
Micky.
Micky who?
Micky won't fit in
the lock.

Knock, knock.
Who's there?
Midas.
Midas who?
Midas well come in.

Knock, knock.
Who's there?
Mike Rowe.
Mike Rowe who?
Mike Rowe wave oven.

Knock, knock.
Who's there?
Miles.
Miles who?
Miles away.

Knock, knock.
Who's there?
Moloch.
Moloch who?
Moloch before you leap!

Knock, knock.
Who's there?
Mortimer.
Mortimer who?
Mortimer than meets
the eye!

116

Knock, knock.
Who's there?
Nicholas.
Nicholas who?
Nicholas girls shouldn't climb trees.

Knock, knock.
Who's there?
Nick.
Nick who?
Nick R. Elastic.

Knock, knock.
Who's there?
Niles.
Niles who?
Niles and a big himmer.

Knock, knock.
Who's there?
Noah.
Noah who?
No, do you?

Knock, knock.
Who's there?
Noel.
Noel who?
Noel in the word Christmas.

Knock, knock.
Who's there?
Olaf.
Olaf who?
Olaf you too.

Knock, knock.
Who's there?
Only Joe.
Only Joe who?
Only Joe King!

Knock, knock.
Who's there?
Orson.
Orson who?
Orson cart.

Knock, knock.
Who's there?
Oswald.
Oswald who?
Oswald my chewing gum.

Knock, knock.
Who's there?
Otto B.
Otto B. who?
Otto B. a law against
people like you!

Knock, knock.
Who's there?
Owen.
Owen who?
Owen will you let me in?

Knock, knock.
Who's there?
Patrick.
Patrick who?
Patrick-ed me into
coming.

Knock, knock.
Who's there?
Paul.
Paul who?
Paul this cracker
with me!

Knock, knock.
Who's there?
Perry.
Perry who?
Perry well, thank you.

Knock, knock.
Who's there?
Percy.
Percy who?
Percy Vere.

Knock, knock.
Who's there?
Peter.
Peter who?
Peter cake.

Knock, knock.
Who's there?
Philip.
Philip who?
Philip my car with petrol.

Knock, knock.
Who's there?
Ramsay.
Ramsay who?
Ramsay 'baaa'.

Knock, knock.
Who's there?
Raoul.
Raoul who?
Raoul up! Raoul up! The
show's about to begin!

Knock, knock.
Who's there?
Ray.
Ray who?
Ray of sunshine!

BAAA!

Knock, knock.
Who's there?
Raymond.
Raymond who?
Raymond me to fix your bell.

Knock, knock.
Who's there?
Reuben.
Reuben who?
Reuben my eyes.

Knock, knock.
Who's there?
Rex.
Rex who?
Rex everything he touches.

Knock, knock.
Who's there?
Rhys.
Rhys who?
Rhys goes well with curry.

Knock, knock.
Who's there?
Robert.
Robert who?
Roberts are taking over the world.

Knock, knock.
Who's there?
Robin.
Robin who?
Robin banks.

Knock, knock.
Who's there?
Robson.
Robson who?
Robson the television?

Knock, knock.
Who's there?
Roger.
Roger who?
Roger ask me that for?

Knock, knock.
Who's there?
Ron.
Ron who?
Ron answer.

Knock, knock.
Who's there?
Ronan.
Ronan who?
Ronan outside.

Knock, knock.
Who's there?
Roy.
Roy who?
Roy L. Flush.

Knock, knock.
Who's there?
Rufus.
Rufus who?
Rufus leaking!

Knock, knock.
Who's there?
Rupert.
Rupert who?
Rupert your left arm in,
your left arm out . . .

Knock, knock.
Who's there?
Sam.
Sam who?
Sam day you'll thank me.

Knock, knock.
Who's there?
Saul.
Saul who?
Saul I know.

Knock, knock.
Who's there?
Scott.
Scott who?
Scott nothing to do
with you.

Knock, knock.
Who's there?
Serge Ickle.
Serge Ickle who?
Serge Ickle gloves.

Knock, knock.
Who's there?
Shaw.
Shaw who?
Shaw is cold out here!

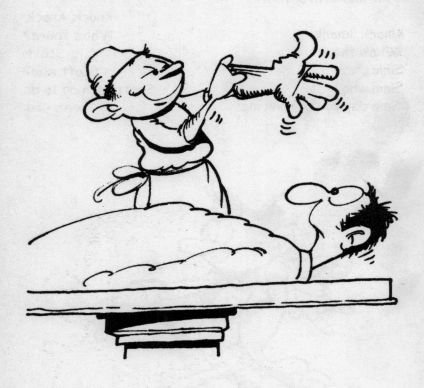

Knock, knock.
Who's there?
Seymour.
Seymour who?
Seymour if you open
the door.

Knock, knock.
Who's there?
Sid.
Sid who?
Sid before, it's me!

Knock, knock.
Who's there?
Simon.
Simon who?
Simon time again I've
told you not to do that.

Knock, knock.
Who's there?
Sir Jerry.
Sir Jerry who?
Sir Jerry to remove
your tonsils.

Knock, knock.
Who's there?
Sir John.
Sir John who?
Sir John took out my
tonsils in the hospital!

Knock, knock.
Who's there?
Sir V. Hugh.
Sir V. Hugh who?
Sir V. Hugh Right!

Knock, knock.
Who's there?
Sonny.
Sonny who?
Sonny me.

Knock, knock.
Who's there?
Spike.
Spike who?
Spike up, I can't
hear you!

Knock, knock.
Who's there?
Stan.
Stan who?
Stan to attention!

Knock, knock.
Who's there?
Stewart.
Stewart who?
Stewart you like, I
don't care!

Knock, knock.
Who's there?
Sven.
Sven who?
Sven are you going to let me in?

Knock, knock.
Who's there?
Terry.
Terry who?
Terry Long the dotted line.

Knock, knock.
Who's there?
Terry Bull.
Terry Bull who?
Terry Bull knock, knock joke.

Knock, knock.
Who's there?
Tex.
Tex who?
Income Tex.

Knock, knock.
Who's there?
Thaddeus.
Thaddeus who?
Thaddeus the thilliest thing I ever heard!

Knock, knock.
Who's there?
Thayer.
Thayer who?
Thayer Thorry.

Knock, knock.
Who's there?
Theodore.
Theodore who?
Theodore won't open.

Knock, knock.
Who's there?
Toby.
Toby who?
Toby or not Toby, that is the question.

Knock, knock.
Who's there?
Tommy.
Tommy who?
Tommy another joke!

Knock, knock.
Who's there?
Travis.
Travis who?
Travis Tee.

Knock, knock.
Who's there?
Tristan.
Tristan who?
Tristan elephant to
remember!

Knock, knock.
Who's there?
Troy.
Troy who?
Troy the bell instead.

Knock, knock.
Who's there?
Turner.
Turner who.
Turner round.

Knock, knock.
Who's there?
Vaughan.
Vaughan who?
Vaughan to hear
another joke?

Knock, knock.
Who's there?
Uriah.
Uriah who?
Keep Uriah on the ball.

Knock, knock.
Who's there?
Vic.
Vic who?
Vic your nose.

Knock, knock.
Who's there?
Victor.
Victor who?
Victor his trousers, so
he can't come out.

Knock, knock.
Who's there?
Walter.
Walter who?
Walter wall carpets.

Knock, knock.
Who's there?
Walter Ring.
Walter Ring who?
Walter Ring the garden.

Knock, knock.
Who's there?
Warren.
Warren who?
Warren you like to know!

Knock, knock.
Who's there?
Watson.
Watson who?
Watson TV?

Knock, knock.
Who's there?
Wayne.
Wayne who?
Wayne or lose, it
doesn't matter!

Knock, knock.
Who's there?
Wes.
Wes who?
Wes-ssuuuup!

Knock, knock.
Who's there?
Wilfred.
Wilfred who?
Wilfred be
arriving later?

Knock, knock.
Who's there?
William.
William who?
William mind your own business.

Knock, knock.
Who's there?
Wilson.
Wilson who?
Wilson body open the door!

Knock, knock.
Who's there?
Worzel?
Worzel who?
It's upstairs, first on the right!

Knock, knock.
Who's there?
Xavier.
Xavier who?
Xavier breath, you're talking rubbish!

Knock, knock.
Who's there?
Yuri.
Yuri who?
Yuri mind me of someone.

Zoo's There?

Knock, knock.
Who's there?
Aardvark.
Aardvark who?
Aardvark a million miles
for one of your smiles.

Knock, knock.
Who's there?
Amoeba.
Amoeba who?
Amoeba wrong, but
haven't we met before?

Knock, knock.
Who's there?
Baboon.
Baboon who?
Baboon burst with
a bang!

Knock, knock.
Who's there?
Baby owl
Baby owl who?
Baby owl see you later,
maybe I won't.

Knock, knock.
Who's there?
Beehive.
Beehive who?
Beehive yourself!

Knock, knock.
Who's there?
Cattle.
Cattle who?
Cattle purr if you
stroke it.

Knock, knock.
Who's there?
Bull.
Bull who?
Bull the chain when
you've finished.

Knock, knock.
Who's there?
Chesterfield.
Chesterfield who?
Chesterfield full
of cows.

Knock, knock.
Who's there?
Cockroach.
Cockroach who?
Cockroach on the
motorway.

Knock, knock.
Who's there?
Cows.
Cows who?
Cows moo, not who.

Knock, knock.
Who's there?
Dinah.
Dinah who?
Dinah-saw.

Knock, knock.
Who's there?
Dinosaur.
Dinosaur who?
Dinosaur you yesterday!

Knock, knock.
Who's there?
Doyouthinkhe?
Doyouthinkhe who?
Doyouthinkhesaurus?

Knock, knock.
Who's there?
Dozen owl go.
Dozen owl go who?
Yes it does.

Knock, knock.
Who's there?
Earwig.
Earwig who?
Earwig go, Earwig go,
Earwig go . . .

Knock, knock.
Who's there?
Ewe.
Ewe who?
Yeah, what do you want?

Knock, knock.
Who's there?
Flea.
Flea who?
Flea blind mice.

Knock, knock.
Who's there?
Furry.
Furry who?
Furry's a jolly good fellow!

Knock, knock.
Who's there?
Giraffe.
Giraffe who?
Girraffe to ask, don't you recognize
my voice?

Knock, knock.
Who's there?
Goose.
Goose who?
Goose who's knocking at the door!

Knock, knock.
Who's there?
Gopher.
Gopher who?
Gopher help – I'm
stuck in the mud.

Knock, knock.
Who's there?
Gorilla.
Gorilla who?
Gorilla sausage.

Knock, knock.
Who's there?
Heifer.
Heifer who?
Heifer beef sandwich!

Knock, knock.
Who's there?
Big Horse.
Big Horse who?
Big Horse I say so!

Knock, knock.
Who's there?
Iguana.
Iguana who?
(sing) "Iguana hold your
hand . . ."

Knock, knock.
Who's there?
Kangaroo.
Kangaroo who?
Kangaroo let me
in please?

Knock, knock.
Who's there?
Lamb.
Lamb who?
Lambada!

Knock, knock.
Who's there?
Lemur.
Lemur who?
Lemur alone!

Knock, knock.
Who's there?
Llama.
Llama who?
Llama just went off,
you're being burgled!

Knock, knock.
Who's there?
Moose.
Moose who?
Moose you ask so many
questions?

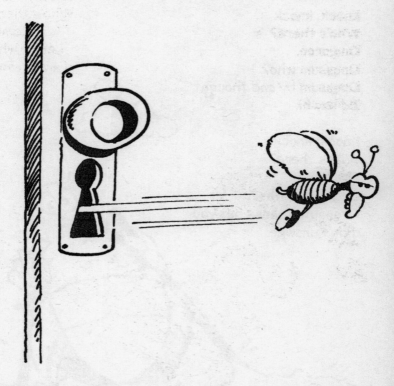

Knock, knock.
Who's there?
Meercat.
Meercat who?
Meercat is better than
your cat!

Knock, knock.
Who's there?
Moth.
Moth who?
Moth get mythelf a
new key.

Knock, knock.
Who's there?
Ocelot.
Ocelot who?
Ocelot of questions,
don't you?

Knock, knock.
Who's there?
Opossum.
Opossum who?
Opossum by and thought
I'd say hi.

Knock, knock.
Who's there?
Orangutan.
Orangutan who?
Orangutan times but you
didn't answer.

Knock, knock.
Who's there?
Owl.
Owl who?
Owl aboard!

Knock, knock.
Who's there?
Oyster.
Oyster who?
Oyster mainsail – land
ahoy!

Knock, knock.
Who's there?
Panda.
Panda who?
Panda-monium!

Knock, knock.
Who's there?
Panther.
Panther who?
Panther no pants, I'm
going thwimming.

Knock, knock.
Who's there?
Parrot.
Parrot who?
Parrot-ly you live here.

Knock, knock.
Who's there?
Phoenix.
Phoenix who?
Phoenix my place, I'm pushing in.

Knock, knock.
Who's there?
Pig.
Pig who?
Pig bad wolf!

Knock, knock.
Who's there?
Python.
Python who?
Pythontennial!

Knock, knock.
Who's there?
Rabbit.
Rabbit who?
Rabbit up carefully, it's a present.

Knock, knock.
Who's there?
Raven.
Raven who?
Raven maniac!

Knock, knock.
Who's there?
R. P.
R. P. who?
R. P. Eagle!

Knock, knock.
Who's there?
Sabre-Tooth.
Sabre-Tooth who?
Sabre-Tooth and put it under your pillow.

Knock, knock.
Who's there?
Sheep.
Sheep who?
Sheep ahoy!

149

Knock, knock.
Who's there?
Spider.
Spider who?
Spider what everyone
says, I like you.

Knock, knock.
Who's there?
Tehran.
Tehran who?
Tehran-o-saurus rex.

Knock, knock.
Who's there?
Termite.
Termite who?
Termite's the night.

Knock, knock.
Who's there?
Terry.
Terry who?
Terry-dactyl.

Knock, knock.
Who's there?
Tick.
Tick who?
Tick 'em up and hand
over your money.

Knock, knock.
Who's there?
Too wit!
Too wit who?
Is there an owl in here?

Knock, knock.
Who's there?
Toad.
Toad who?
Toad you before,
remember?

Knock, knock.
Who's there?
Toucan.
Toucan who?
Toucan play at
this game.

151

Knock, knock.
Who's there?
Turtle.
Turtle who?
Turtle come out in
the wash!

Knock, knock.
Who's there?
Udder.
Udder who?
Udder destruction!

Knock, knock.
Who's there?
Viper.
Viper who?
Viper your nose.

Knock, knock.
Who's there?
Wallaby.
Wallaby who?
Wallaby-ootiful day!

Knock, knock.
Who's there?
Walrus.
Walrus who?
Why do Walrus ask silly
questions?

Knock, knock.
Who's there?
Wasp.
Wasp who?
Wasp with you?

Knock, knock.
Who's there?
Weasel.
Weasel who?
(sing) "Weasel while you
work..."

Knock, knock.
Who's there?
Weevil.
Weevil who?
Weevil survive!

153

Knock, knock.
Who's there?
Whale.
Whale who?
Whale you let me in?

Knock, knock.
Who's there?
Wolf.
Wolf who?
Wolf from a sheep.

Knock, knock.
Who's there?
Wombat.
Wombat who?
Wombat is better than none!

Knock, knock.
Who's there?
Worm.
Worm who?
Worm in here, isn't it?

Knock, knock.
Who's there?
Yeti.
Yeti who?
Yeti nother knock, knock joke!

All Around the World

Knock, knock.
Who's there?
Aberdeen.
Aberdeen who?
Aberdeen to Scotland?

Knock, knock.
Who's there?
Abyssinia.
Abyssinia who?
Abyssinia soon.

Knock, knock.
Who's there?
Adelaide.
Adelaide who?
Adelaide an egg!

Knock, knock.
Who's there?
Afghan.
Afghan who?
Afghan away and I'm not coming back!

Knock, knock.
Who's there?
Afghanistan.
Afghanistan who?
Afghanistan here all day
until you open the door!

Knock, knock.
Who's there?
Alaska.
Alaska who?
Alaska one more time.

Knock, knock.
Who's there?
Amarillo.
Amarillo who?
Amarillo nice person!

Knock, knock.
Who's there?
Andalusia.
Andalusia who?
I'd like to take you
somewhere Andalusia!

Knock, knock.
Who's there?
Asia.
Asia who?
Asia mother in?

Knock, knock.
Who's there?
Babylon.
Babylon who?
Babylon, I'm not
listening anyway!

Knock, knock.
Who's there?
Avon.
Avon who?
Avon to be alone.

Knock, knock.
Who's there?
Belize.
Belize who?
Belize yourself then.

Knock, knock.
Who's there?
Berlin.
Berlin who?
Berlin a kettle.

Knock, knock.
Who's there?
Bolivia.
Bolivia who?
Bolivia me, I'm telling
the truth!

Knock, knock.
Who's there?
Bolton.
Bolton who?
Bolton the door.

Knock, knock.
Who's there?
Bosnia.
Bosnia who?
Bosnia bell here earlier?

Knock, knock.
Who's there?
Brighton.
Brighton who?
I'm up Brighton early to
see you!

Knock, knock.
Who's there?
Bristol.
Bristol who?
Bristol my aching heart!

Knock, knock.
Who's there?
Budapest.
Budapest who?
You're nothing Budapest!

Knock, knock.
Who's there?
Cairo.
Cairo who?
Cairo-practor

Knock, knock.
Who's there?
Canada.
Canada who?
Can-Ada come out to play?

Knock, knock.
Who's there?
Catania.
Catania who?
Catania horse and ride!

Knock, knock.
Who's there?
Cologne.
Cologne who?
Cologne Ranger.

Knock, knock.
Who's there?
Congo.
Congo who?
Congo out, it's raining!

Knock, knock.
Who's there?
Crete.
Crete who?
Crete to see you.

Knock, knock.
Who's there?
Czech.
Czech who?
Czech before you open the door.

Knock, knock.
Who's there?
Dakar.
Dakar who?
Dakar has a flat tyre!

Knock, knock.
Who's there?
Dakota.
Dakota who?
Dakota many colours.

Knock, knock.
Who's there?
Damascus.
Damascus who?
Damascus slipping off
da face.

Knock, knock.
Who's there?
Darwin.
Darwin who?
I'll be Darwin you
need me!

Knock, knock.
Who's there?
Doncaster.
Doncaster who?
Doncaster as Juliet, but
she was rubbish.

Knock, knock.
Who's there?
Dublin.
Dublin who?
Dublin up with laughter.

163

Knock, knock.
Who's there?
Dutch.
Dutch who?
Dutch me and
I'll scream!

Knock, knock.
Who's there?
Genoa.
Genoa who?
Genoa nother knock,
knock joke?

Knock, knock.
Who's there?
Europe.
Europe who?
Europe-ning the
door soon?

Knock, knock.
Who's there?
Glasgow.
Glasgow who?
Glasgow to the movies.

Knock, knock.
Who's there?
Haiti.
Haiti who?
Haiti-ting vegetables.

Knock, knock.
Who's there?
Hanover.
Hanover who?
Hanover your money!

Knock, knock.
Who's there?
Hawaii.
Hawaii who?
I'm fine, thank you.

Knock, knock.
Who's there?
India.
India who?
India night-time I go
to sleep.

Knock, knock.
Who's there?
Ireland.
Ireland who?
Ireland you some money
if you promise to pay
me back.

Knock, knock.
Who's there?
Indonesia.
Indonesia who?
You make me weak
Indonesia!

Knock, knock.
Who's there?
Iran.
Iran who?
Iran away when you
answered before.

Knock, knock.
Who's there?
Italian.
Italian who?
Italian you for the last
time, let me in!

Knock, knock.
Who's there?
Jamaica.
Jamaica who?
Jamaica mistake?

Knock, knock.
Who's there?
Java.
Java who?
Java doorbell?

Knock, knock.
Who's there?
Kent.
Kent who?
Kent you tell?

Knock, knock.
Who's there?
Kenya.
Kenya who?
Kenya keep the noise down?

Knock, knock.
Who's there?
Kuwait.
Kuwait who?
Kuwait here, I'll go for help.

Knock, knock.
Who's there?
Lisbon.
Lisbon who?
Lisbon away a long time.

Knock, knock.
Who's there?
London.
London who?
London and two to go.

Knock, knock.
Who's there?
Mecca.
Mecca who?
Mecca me an offer I can't refuse.

Knock, knock.
Who's there?
Norway.
Norway who?
Norway to treat a lady.

Knock, knock.
Who's there?
Oslo.
Oslo who?
Oslo down, you're going
too fast!

Knock, knock.
Who's there?
Oxford.
Oxford who?
You Oxford it!

Knock, knock.
Who's there?
Paris.
Paris who?
Paris the pepper please.

Knock, knock.
Who's there?
Perth.
Perth who?
Perth the parthel.

Knock, knock.
Who's there?
Quebec.
Quebec who?
Quebec where we
started! Knock, knock . . .

Knock, knock.
Who's there?
Prussia.
Prussia who?
Prussia cooker.

Knock, knock.
Who's there?
Rumania.
Rumania who?
Rumania for one more?

Knock, knock.
Who's there?
Russia.
Russia who?
Never Russia good thing!

Knock, knock.
Who's there?
Samoa.
Samoa who?
Samoa these jokes and
I'm going to scream!

Knock, knock.
Who's there?
Sicily.
Sicily who?
Sicily question!

Knock, knock.
Who's there?
Spain.
Spain who?
Spain to keep knocking.

Knock, knock.
Who's there?
Toronto.
Toronto who?
I have Toronto the shops for some chocolate.

Knock, knock.
Who's there?
Sweden.
Sweden who?
Sweden sour pork.

Knock, knock.
Who's there?
Uruguay.
Uruguay who?
Uruguay your way and I'll go mine!

Knock, knock.
Who's there?
Tibet.
Tibet who?
It's time I went Tibet!

172

Knock, knock.
Who's there?
Venice.
Venice who?
Venice this going to end?

Knock, knock.
Who's there?
Winchester.
Winchester who?
Winchester comes, tell him I called.

Knock, knock.
Who's there?
Yukon.
Yukon who?
Yukon talk to me like that!

What's For Dinner?

Knock, knock.
Who's there?
Almond.
Almond who?
Almond the side of the Law!

Knock, knock.
Who's there?
Apple.
Apple who?
Apple and you push!

Knock, knock.
Who's there?
Aubergine.
Aubergine who?
Aubergine you in court!

Knock, knock.
Who's there?
Avocado.
Avocado who?
Avocado on much longer!

Knock, knock.
Who's there?
Bacon.
Bacon who?
Bacon a cake for your
birthday.

Knock, knock.
Who's there?
Banana.
Banana who?
Banana messages for
me?

Knock, knock.
Who's there?
Banana.
Banana who?
Knock, knock.
Who's there?
Banana.
Banana who?
Knock, knock.
Who's there?
Banana.
Banana who?

Knock, knock.
Who's there?
Orange
Orange who?
Orange you glad I
didn't say banana?

176

Knock, knock.
Who's there?
Beef.
Beef who?
Beef fair!

Knock, knock.
Who's there?
Boxer.
Boxer who?
Boxer chocolates!

Knock, knock.
Who's there?
Beetroot.
Beetroot who?
Beetroot yourself.

Knock, knock.
Who's there?
Buck and Ham.
Buck and Ham who?
Buck and Ham Palace.

Knock, knock.
Who's there?
Butter.
Butter who?
Butter hurry up, I need
the toilet now!

Knock, knock.
Who's there?
Cantaloupe.
Cantaloupe who?
Cantaloupe today, maybe
next week!

Knock, knock.
Who's there?
Cashew.
Cashew who?
Cashew look through the
letterbox?

Knock, knock.
Who's there?
Cereal.
Cereal who?
Cereal pleasure to
meet you.

Knock, knock.
Who's there?
Cheese.
Cheese who?
Cheese a jolly good
fellow.

Knock, knock.
Who's there?
Chicken.
Chicken who?
Chicken your pockets —
your keys are in there.

Knock, knock.
Who's there?
Cucumber.
Cucumber who?
Cucumber and say that!

Knock, knock.
Who's there?
Doughnut.
Doughnut who?
Doughnut open the door, whatever you do.

Knock, knock.
Who's there?
Figs.
Figs who?
Figs the bell.

Knock, knock.
Who's there?
Fish.
Fish who?
Bless you!

Knock, knock.
Who's there?
Fudge.
Fudge who?
Fudge up and make room.

Knock, knock.
Who's there?
Give Pizza.
Give Pizza who?
Give Pizza chance!

Knock, knock.
Who's there?
Halibut.
Halibut who?
Halibut letting me in?

Knock, knock.
Who's there?
Irish Stew.
Irish Stew who?
Irish Stew would open the door!

Knock, knock.
Who's there?
Jam.
Jam who?
Jam mind letting me in?

Knock, knock.
Who's there?
Juice.
Juice who?
Juice still want to know?

Knock, knock.
Who's there?
Ketchup.
Ketchup who?
Ketchup with me later
and I'll tell you.

Knock, knock.
Who's there?
Kipper.
Kipper who?
Kipper your hands to
yourself.

Knock, knock.
Who's there?
Lettuce.
Lettuce who?
Lettuce in and we'll tell
you.

Knock, knock.
Who's there?
Marietta.
Marietta who?
Marietta whole cake!

Knock, knock.
Who's there?
Mayonnaise.
Mayonnaise who?
(sing) "Mayonnaise have
seen the glory of the
coming of the Lord . . ."

Knock, knock.
Who's there?
Marsha.
Marsha who?
Marsha Mallow!

Knock, knock.
Who's there?
Melon.
Melon who?
Melon-dry will be dry
soon.

183

Knock, knock.
Who's there?
Mint.
Mint who?
Mint to tell you earlier.

Knock, knock.
Who's there?
Muffin.
Muffin who?
Muffin you too.

Knock, knock.
Who's there?
Mustard.
Mustard who?
Mustard lost my key.

Knock, knock.
Who's there?
Oil.
Oil who?
Oil be seeing you!

Knock, knock.
Who's there?
Omelette.
Omelette who?
Omelette smarter than
I look!

Knock, knock.
Who's there?
Onion.
Onion who?
Onion-ing for you!

Knock, knock.
Who's there?
Pasta.
Pasta who?
Pasta salt please.

Knock, knock.
Who's there?
Peas.
Peas who?
Peas to meet you.

Knock, knock.
Who's there?
Pecan.
Pecan who?
(sing) "Pecan work it out, Pecan work it out . . ."

Knock, knock.
Who's there?
Plums.
Plums who?
Plums me you won't tell?

Knock, knock.
Who's there?
Pretzel.
Pretzel who?
Pretzel call again later!

Knock, knock.
Who's there?
Pudding.
Pudding who?
Pudding my best foot forward!

Knock, knock.
Who's there?
Quiche.
Quiche who?
Quiche me quick!

Knock, knock.
Who's there?
Rice.
Rice who?
Rice you to the end of the road!

Knock, knock.
Who's there?
Roland.
Roland who?
Roland butter, please, waiter.

Knock, knock.
Who's there?
Ross.
Ross who?
Ross Beef!

Knock, knock.
Who's there?
Saffron.
Saffron who?
Saffron a chair and it
collapsed!

Knock, knock.
Who's there?
Shallot.
Shallot who?
Shallot of fuss over
nothing!

Knock, knock.
Who's there?
Sherbert.
Sherbert who?
Sherbert to his room.

Knock, knock.
Who's there?
Sir Lloyd.
Sir Lloyd who?
Sir Lloyd Steak, medium
rare.

Knock, knock.
Who's there?
Swede.
Swede who?
Swede of you to ask.

Knock, knock.
Who's there?
Truffle.
Truffle who?
Sorry to Truffle you!

Knock, knock.
Who's there?
Toast.
Toast who?
Toast were the days!

Knock, knock.
Who's there?
Turnip.
Turnip who?
Turnip the volume.

Knock, knock.
Who's there?
Wafer.
Wafer who?
Wafer me at the corner.

Knock, knock.
Who's there?
Walnuts.
Walnuts who?
Walnuts around here!

Knock, knock.
Who's there?
Water.
Water who?
Water you waiting for,
let me in!

Knock, knock.
Who's there?
X.
X who?
X for breakfast.

Knock, knock.
Who's there?
Yoghurt.
Yoghurt who?
Yoghurt to be joking!

Famous
People

Knock, knock.
Who's there?
Abe Lincoln
Abe Lincoln who?
Abe Lincoln yellow light
means slow down!

Knock, knock.
Who's there?
Achilles.
Achilles who?
Achilles mosquitoes with
a swatter!

Knock, knock.
Who's there?
Amber Lynn
Amber Lynn who?
Amber Lynn had 'er 'ed
chopped off!

Knock, knock.
Who's there?
Apollo G.
Apollo G. who?
Apollo G. accepted!

Knock, knock.
Who's there?
Athena.
Athena who?
Athena some place before, haven't I?

Knock, knock.
Who's there?
Bach
Bach who?
Bach of sweets.

Knock, knock.
Who's there?
Buddha.
Buddha who?
Buddha this slice of bread for me.

Knock, knock.
Who's there?
Byron.
Byron who?
Byron get one free!

Knock, knock.
Who's there?
Caesar.
Caesar who?
Caesar quickly before she escapes!

Knock, knock.
Who's there?
Caesar.
Caesar who?
Caesar jolly good fellow!

Knock, knock.
Who's there?
Darth Vader.
Darth Vader who?
Darth Vader cookie crumbles!

Knock, knock.
Who's there?
Elvis.
Elvis who?
Elvis seeing you sometime.

Knock, knock.
Who's there?
Eumenides.
Eumenides who?
Eumenides trousers.

Knock, knock.
Who's there?
Euripides.
Euripides who?
Euripides, you pay for a
new pair.

Knock, knock.
Who's there?
Goliath.
Goliath who?
Goliath down, you need a
retht!

Knock, knock.
Who's there?
Handel.
Handel who?
Handel with care.

Knock, knock.
Who's there?
Haydn.
Haydn who?
Haydn the shed.

Knock, knock.
Who's there?
Judah.
Judah who?
Judah known by now if
you'd opened the door.

Knock, knock.
Who's there?
Hiawatha.
Hiawatha who?
Hiawatha boxther, but
now I've retired!

Knock, knock.
Who's there?
Minerva.
Minerva who?
Minerva-s wreck.

Knock, knock.
Who's there?
Mozart.
Mozart who?
Mozart is in museums.

Knock, knock.
Who's there?
Nero.
Nero who?
Nero far.

Knock, knock.
Who's there?
Odysseus.
Odysseus who?
Odysseus is the last
straw!

Knock, knock.
Who's there?
Plato.
Plato who?
Plato fish and chips!

Knock, knock.
Who's there?
Ptolemy.
Ptolemy who?
Ptolemy another joke!

Knock, knock.
Who's there?
Thor.
Thor who?
I. M. Thor all over.

Knock, knock.
Who's there?
Tom Sawyer.
Tom Sawyer who?
Tom Sawyer underpants!

Knock, knock.
Who's there?
Tudors.
Tudors who?
Tudors to choose from,
so I knocked on yours.

Bits and Bodies

Knock, knock.
Who's there?
Big Toe.
Big Toe who?
Big Toe right house then.

Knock, knock.
Who's there?
Buttock.
Buttock who?
Buttock cups are yellow.

Knock, knock.
Who's there?
Chest.
Chest who?
Chest open the door.

Knock, knock.
Who's there?
Chin.
Chin who?
Chin television!

Knock, knock.
Who's there?
Ears.
Ears who?
Ears looking at you, kid.

Knock, knock.
Who's there?
Elbow.
Elbow who?
Elbow seeing you!

Knock, knock.
Who's there?
Eyebrow.
Eyebrow who?
Eyebrow to your superior knowledge.

Knock, knock.
Who's there?
Eyelash.
Eyelash who?
Eyelash poor Yorick, I knew him Horatio.

Knock, knock.
Who's there?
Finger.
Finger who?
Finger just broke your
door knocker.

Knock, knock.
Who's there?
Finger Nail.
Finger Nail who?
Finger Nail should fix it!

Knock, knock.
Who's there?
Hair.
Hair who?
Hair today, gone
tomorrow.

Knock, knock.
Who's there?
Hair Combs.
Hair Combs who?
Hair Combs the bride!

Knock, knock.
Who's there?
Kidney.
Kidney who?
Kidney open the door please?

Knock, knock.
Who's there?
Nose.
Nose who?
Nose surrender!

Knock, knock.
Who's there?
Liver.
Liver who?
Liver let live.

Knock, knock.
Who's there?
Shoulder.
Shoulder who?
Shoulder the highesht bidder!

Knock, knock.
Who's there?
Spleen.
Spleen who?
Spleen nice knowing you.

Knock, knock.
Who's there?
Teeth.
Teeth who?
Teeth ent it obviouth?

Knock, knock.
Who's there?
Thighs.
Thighs who?
Thighs the limit.

Knock, knock.
Who's there?
Throat.
Throat who?
Throat to me!

204

Knock, knock.
Who's there?
Thumb.
Thumb who?
Thumb day my printh will come.

Knock, knock.
Who's there?
Toothache.
Toothache who?
(sing) "Toothache the high road and I'll take the low road . . ."

Knock, knock.
Who's there?
Tummy.
Tummy who?
Tummy you will always be special!

Knock, knock.
Who's there?
Wart.
Wart who?
Wart am I waiting for? Let me in!

Ring! Ring!

Knock, knock.
Who's there?
B4.
B4 who?
B4 I get really annoyed, open the door!

Knock, knock.
Who's there?
Caitlin.
Caitlin who?
Caitlin you my mobile phone.

Knck, knck.
Whz thr?
C2.
C2 who?
C2 it you let me in soon.

Knock, knock.
Who's there?
Cindy.
Cindy who?
Cindy me a text message.

Knock, knock.
Who's there?
Ericsson.
Ericsson who?
Ericsson the phone.

Knck, knck.
Whz thr?
i 1 2.
i 1 2 who?
(sing) "i 1 2 hold your hand . . ."

Knock, knock.
Who's there?
Imogen.
Imogen who?
Imogen life without your mobile.

Knock, knock.
Who's there?
Nokia.
Nokia who?
Nokia, so hadda to knock!

Knock, knock.
Who's there?
Orange.
Orange who?
Orange you glad you got a mobile phone?

Knock, knock.
Who's there?
Phone.
Phone who?
Phone I'd known it was you!

Knck, knck.
Whz thr?
1.
1 who?
121.

Knck, knck.
Whz thr?
NE1.
NE1 who?
NE1 you like.

Pick a
Colour

Knock, knock.
Who's there?
Black.
Black who?
Black of ice!

Knock, knock.
Who's there?
Brown.
Brown who?
Brown bread.

Knock, knock.
Who's there?
Blue
Blue who?
Cheer up!

Knock, knock.
Who's there?
Green.
Green who?
Green and bear it.

Knock, knock.
Who's there?
Grey.
Grey who?
Grey-t balls of fire.

Knock, knock.
Who's there?
Mauve.
Mauve who?
Mauve over, darling.

Knock, knock.
Who's there?
Pink.
Pink who?
Pink keeping busy?

Knock, knock.
Who's there?
Red.
Red who?
Red any good books
lately?

Knock, knock.
Who's there?
Violet.
Violet who?
Violet the dog out, will
you take it for a walk?

Knock, knock.
Who's there?
White.
White who?
White in the thick of it.

Knock, knock.
Who's there?
Yellow.
Yellow who?
Yellow down dirty rat!

Whoooo's There?

Knock, knock.
Who's there?
Aaron.
Aaron who?
Aaron your palms!

Knock, knock.
Who's there?
Alfred.
Alfred who?
Alfred of the dark.

Knock, knock.
Who's there?
Alistair.
Alistair who?
Alistair-s are creaking!

Knock, knock.
Who's there?
Amanda.
Amanda who?
Amanda the table.

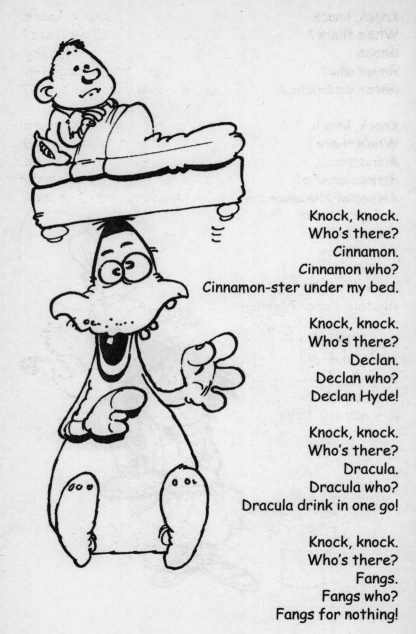

Knock, knock.
Who's there?
Cinnamon.
Cinnamon who?
Cinnamon-ster under my bed.

Knock, knock.
Who's there?
Declan.
Declan who?
Declan Hyde!

Knock, knock.
Who's there?
Dracula.
Dracula who?
Dracula drink in one go!

Knock, knock.
Who's there?
Fangs.
Fangs who?
Fangs for nothing!

Knock, knock.
Who's there?
Ghost.
Ghost who?
Ghost is clear!

Knock, knock.
Who's there?
Gruesome.
Gruesome who?
I wanted some flowers,
so I gruesome!

Knock, knock.
Who's there?
Howling.
Howling who?
Howling must I wait?

Knock, knock.
Who's there?
Hugh.
Hugh who?
Hugh's afraid of ghosts?

Knock, knock.
Who's there?
Hugo.
Hugo who?
Hugo first, I'm
frightened!

Knock, knock.
Who's there?
Ooze.
Ooze who?
Ooze there?

Knock, knock.
Who's there?
Lucretia.
Lucretia who?
Lucretia from the Blue
Lagoon.

Knock, knock.
Who's there?
Paul.
Paul who?
Paul-tergeist!

Knock, knock.
Who's there?
Spectre.
Spectre who?
Spectre I'll see you later!

Knock, knock.
Who's there?
Spook.
Spook who?
Spook when you're spooken to!

Knock, knock.
Who's there?
Thumping green.
Thumping green who?
Thumping green and slimy just crawled up your leg!

Knock, knock.
Who's there?
Weirdo.
Weirdo who?
Weirdo you think you're going?

Knock, knock.
Who's there?
Werewolf.
Werewolf who?
Werewolf for cleaning
saucepans!

Knock, knock.
Who's there?
Wyden.
Wyden who?
Wyden you tell me you
were a werewolf?

Teacher! Teacher!

Knock, knock.
Who's there?
Althea.
Althea who?
Althea after school.

Knock, knock.
Who's there?
Brooke.
Brooke who?
Brooke Shelf!

Knock, knock.
Who's there?
Colleen.
Colleen who?
Colleen up your desk, it's messy!

Knock, knock.
Who's there?
Don Juan.
Don Juan who?
Don Juan to go to school today?

Knock, knock.
Who's there?
Exam.
Exam who?
Exam-wich!

Knock, knock.
Who's there?
Gladys.
Gladys who?
Gladys the end of term!

Knock, knock.
Who's there?
Josette.
Josette who?
Josette down and be quiet!

Knock, knock.
Who's there?
Justin.
Justin who?
Justin time, the bell's rung!

223

Knock, knock.
Who's there?
Lesson.
Lesson who?
Lesson to me when I'm talking!

Knock, knock.
Who's there?
School Dinner.
School Dinner who?
School Dinner here, close the window!

Knock, knock.
Who's there?
Taught.
Taught who?
Taught you'd never ask!

Knock, knock.
Who's there?
Vanessa.
Vanessa who?
Vanessa lesson is Maths!

$$\frac{2}{106} \times 3^7 =$$

$$\frac{17}{9} \div 17 =$$

$$\frac{2001}{93.3} \div \frac{2600}{19} \left(9 \times 7\right)^2$$
$$=$$

Sing a Song

Knock, knock.
Who's there?
Adam Mick.
Adam Mick who?
Adam Mick Kitten!

Knock, knock.
Who's there?
Amahl.
Amahl who?
(sing) "Amahl shook up,
uh-huh-huh . . ."

Knock, knock.
Who's there?
Al and Edith.
Al and Edith who?
(sing) "Al and Edith love . . ."

Knock, knock.
Who's there?
Baby Faith.
Baby Faith who?
(sing) "Baby Faith, you've
got the cutestht little
Baby Faith . . ."

226

Knock, knock.
Who's there?
Barbara.
Barbara who?
(sing) "Barbara black sheep, have you any wool?"

Knock, knock.
Who's there?
Britches.
Britches who?
(sing) "London Britches falling down . . ."

Knock, knock.
Who's there?
Britney.
Britney who?
Knock, knock.
Who's there?
Britney.
Britney who?
(sing) "Oops, I've done it again."

Knock, knock.
Who's there?
B*.
B* who?
B*Witched!

Knock, knock.
Who's there?
Dancer.
Dancer who?
(sing) "Dancer my friend,
is blowing in the wind . . ."

Knock, knock.
Who's there?
Dee Wallace.
Dee Wallace who?
(sing) "Dee Wallace came
tumbling down . . ."

Knock, knock.
Who's there?
Diane Kilburn.
Diane Kilburn who?
(sing) "Diane Kilburn's
connected to the foot
bone . . ."

Knock, knock.
Who's there?
Diesel.
Diesel who?
(sing) "Diesel man, he
played one, he played knick
knack on my drum . . ."

Knock, knock.
Who's there?
Donovan.
Donovan who?
Donovan to hear another word out of you!

Knock, knock.
Who's there?
Eloise.
Eloise who?
(sing) "Eloise release me, let me go . . ."

Knock, knock.
Who's there?
Emma.
Emma who?
Emma Nemm!

Knock, knock.
Who's there?
Few don't.
Few don't who?
(sing) "Few don't know me by now . . ."

Knock, knock.
Who's there?
Freddie.
Freddie who?
(sing) "Freddie or not, here I come, you can't hide . . ."

Knock, knock.
Who's there?
G. Knee
G. Knee who?
(sing) "G. Knee in a bottle . . ."

Knock, knock.
Who's there?
Hannah.
Hannah who?
(sing) "Hannah partridge in a pear tree . . ."

Knock, knock.
Who's there?
Hey.
Hey who?
(sing) "Hey who, hey who, it's off to work we go . . ."

Knock, knock.
Who's there?
Iona.
Iona who?
(sing) "Iona have eyes
for you . . ."

Knock, knock.
Who's there?
Irma.
Irma who?
(sing) "Irma lumberjack
and I'm OK . . ."

Knock, knock.
Who's there?
Lucinda.
Lucinda who?
(sing) "Lucinda the sky
with diamonds . . ."

Knock, knock.
Who's there?
Mindy.
Mindy who?
(sing) "Mindy mood for
dancing . . ."

Knock, knock.
Who's there?
Mis-teeq.
Mis-teeq who?
Mis-teeq is overcooked.

Knock, knock.
Who's there?
Ray.
Ray who?
(sing) "Ray drops keep falling on my head . . ."

Knock, knock.
Who's there?
Raoul.
Raoul who?
(sing) "Raoul out the barrel . . ."

Knock, knock.
Who's there?
Rhoda.
Rhoda who?
(sing) "I'm on the Rhoda nowhere . . ."

Knock, knock.
Who's there?
Sam and Janet.
Sam and Janet who?
(sing) "Sam and Janet
evening . . ."

Knock, knock.
Who's there?
Sid.
Sid who?
(sing) "Sid down, you're
rocking the boat . . ."

Knock, knock.
Who's there?
Sondheim.
Sondheim who?
Sondheim soon we'll
meet again.

Knock, knock.
Who's there?
Stan.
Stan who?
(sing) "Stan by your man . . ."

Knock, knock.
Who's there?
Tara.
Tara who?
(sing) "Tara-raboomdeeay,
Tara-raboomdeeay!"

Knock, knock.
Who's there?
Wayne.
Wayne who?
(sing) "Wayne dwops keep
falling on my head . . ."

Knock, knock.
Who's there?
Wendy.
Wendy who?
(sing) "Wendy saints go
marching in . . ."

Knock, knock.
Who's there?
Wire.
Wire who?
(sing) "Wire we waiting,
wire we waiting . . . ?"

Double Trouble

Knock, knock.
Who's there?
Alda and Alda.
Alda and Alda who?
I'm getting Alda and Alda waiting here!

Knock, knock.
Who's there?
Ben and Anna.
Ben and Anna who?
Ben and Anna split with ice cream!

Knock, knock.
Who's there?
Carmen or Cohen.
Carmen or Cohen who?
You don't know whether you're Carmen or Cohen!

Knock, knock.
Who's there?
Harv and Hugh.
Harv and Hugh who?
Harv and Hugh got a clue?

Knock, knock.
Who's there?
Heywood Hugh Harry.
Heywood Hugh Harry who?
Heywood Hugh Harry up and open the door!

Knock, knock.
Who's there?
John and Cilla.
John and Cilla who?
John the Navy and Cilla seven seas!

Knock, knock.
Who's there?
Ollie or Rex.
Ollie or Rex who?
Don't put Ollie or Rex in one basket.

Knock, knock.
Who's there?
Oscar and Greta.
Oscar and Greta who?
Oscar silly question and Greta silly answer!

Knock, knock.
Who's there?
Saul and Terry.
Saul and Terry who?
Saul and Terry
confinement.

Knock, knock.
Who's there?
Stan and Bea.
Stan and Bea who?
Stan Dupp and Bea
Counted!

Lucky Dip

Knock, knock.
Who's there?
A widow.
A widow who?
A widow birdie.

Knock, knock
Who's there?
Autumn.
Autumn who?
You Autumn mind your
own business!

Knock, knock.
Who's there?
Amen.
Amen who?
Amen trouble deep!

Knock, knock.
Who's there?
Bless.
Bless who?
I didn't sneeze!

Knock, knock.
Who's there?
Canoe.
Canoe who?
Canoe lend me a fiver?

Knock, knock.
Who's there?
Chess game.
Chess game who?
Chess game to say hello.

Knock, knock.
Who's there?
Derision.
Derision who?
Derision room in this
town for both of us!

Knock, knock.
Who's there?
Disguise.
Disguise who?
Disguise the limit!

Knock, knock.
Who's there?
Dishes.
Dishes who?
Dishes the police, we
have you surrounded.

Knock, knock.
Who's there?
Duke.
Duke who?
Duke come here often?

Knock, knock.
Who's there?
Easter.
Easter who?
Easter anybody home?

Knock, knock.
Who's there?
Festival.
Festival who?
Festival open the door,
then I'll tell you!

Knock, knock.
Who's there?
I've done a per.
I've done a per who?
Charming!

Knock, knock.
Who's there?
Juicy.
Juicy who?
Juicy what I see?

Knock, knock.
Who's there?
Little old lady.
Little old lady who?
I didn't know you could yodel.

Knock, knock.
Who's there?
Mrs Ippy.
Mrs Ippey who?
Mrs Ippey River.

Knock, knock.
Who's there?
Nurse.
Nurse who?
Nurse sense in talking to you!

Knock, knock.
Who's there?
Punch.
Punch who?
Why, what have I ever done to you?

Knock, knock.
Who's there?
Sarong and Sari.
Sarong and Sari who?
Sarong house, Sari.

Knock, knock.
Who's there?
Says.
Says who?
Says me,
that's who!

Knock, knock.
Who's there?
Spell.
Spell who?
W-H-O.

Knock, knock.
Who's there?
Thermos.
Thermos who?
Thermos be an
easier way!

Knock, knock.
Who's there?
Thumping.
Thumping who?
Thumping's jutht
knocked my teef out.

Knock, knock.
Who's there?
Trigger.
Trigger who?
Trigger treat!

Knock, knock.
Who's there?
Vacancy.
Vacancy who?
Vacancy you hiding
in there!

Knock, knock.
Who's there?
Virtue.
Virtue who?
Virtue get those big
brown eyes?

Knock, knock.
Who's there?
Violins.
Violins who?
Violins will get you
nowhere!

Knock, knock.
Who's there?
Waddle.
Waddle who?
Waddle you give me to
go away?

Knock, knock.
Who's there?
Wade.
Wade who?
Wade-ing Room

Knock, knock.
Who's there?
Waiter.
Waiter who?
Waiter round and
you'll see!

Knock, knock.
Who's there?
Who who.
Who who who?
What's so funny?

Knock, knock.
Who's there?
Wooden shoe.
Wooden shoe who?
Wooden shoe like
to know!

Knock, knock.
Who's there?
Wound.
Wound who?
Wound and wound the wugged wock the wugged wascal wan.

Knock, knock.
Who's there?
Yah.
Yah who?
Ride 'em cowboy!

Knock, knock.
Who's there?
You're unaware.
You're unaware who?
Your unaware has a hole in it!

Knock, knock.
Who's there?
Zinc.
Zinc who?
Zinc or swim.